Crap
MPs *

* *In our opinion*

Crap
MPs*

Bendor Grosvenor &
Geoffrey Hicks

* In our opinion

The Friday Project
An imprint of HarperCollinsPublishers
77–85 Fulham Palace Road
Hammersmith, London W6 8JB
www.harpercollins.co.uk

Love this book? www.bookarmy.com

First published in Great Britain by The Friday Project in 2009
Copyright © Bendor Grosvenor and Geoffrey Hicks 2009

1

Bendor Grosvenor and Geoffrey Hicks assert the moral right to
be identified as the author of this work

A catalogue record for this book
is available from the British Library

978-0-00-734868-8

Typeset by Leo Nickolls

Printed and bound in Spain by
Gráficas Estella

This book was written on an impulse in August, and published just two months later. My special thanks are therefore due to The Friday Project and HarperCollins for their enthusiasm and support, in particular Victoria Barnsley and Scott Pack. I am also grateful to Corinna Harrod, Robin Harvie, Caitlin Doyle, Leo Nickolls, Chris Gurney and the various lawyers we have consulted for working so hard to turn an idea into reality. I would like to thank my co-author Geoffrey Hicks for the prompt delivery of his excellent text, and for letting me interrupt his summer. Finally, although it must be deeply unromantic to dedicate a book called 'crap' to someone, this is for Edite.

Bendor Grosvenor

Introduction

Some people say that the expenses scandal of 2009 has done more damage to our political system than any other single episode in modern British history. Actually, the reverse is true. Thanks to the recent revelations of fraud, arrogance and incompetence, we are now more aware of the shortcomings of our leaders than ever before. We are governed by a uniquely crap generation of politicians. And now that we know, we can begin to do something about it.

But just how bad are today's MPs, compared with their predecessors? This book attempts to answer that question by looking at MPs from the sixteenth century to the present day. It includes the murderous, the corrupt, the perverted and the merely useless. We have chosen forty — about one-quarter of whom are made up of current MPs. Only three of the forty are women. Strangely, there are eight Johns. The criteria for crapness are not scientific, and are based (libel lawyers, please note) purely on our own opinion. Some may wonder at the absence of those who ended up mired in political manure, such as John Major, James Callaghan, or even our own Gordon Brown, but political failure does not qualify anyone for this list. Individual failings do.

Symbols

A guide to the symbols used throughout this book. They are not to be taken entirely seriously.

Money

Dodgy Friends

Booze

Burning Heretics

Blackmail

Crimes against Xmas Cards

Prison

Bigot

Theft

Traitor

ABC
Crimes against the English Language

Vandal

Terrible Decision

Liar

Nutter

Dodgy Photos

Foreign Policy

Thatcherism

Skiving

Done a Runner

Inappropriate Animal Behaviour

Resignation

Potty Mouth

Murder

Sex

Kicked Out

Slave Trade

Forgery

Drugs

Philistine

Too Litigious to have a Symbol

1

'It was never liked by the ducks and is now in storage.'

Sir Peter Viggers

(b.1938) Conservative, Gosport, 1974–

£££ 🐄 👢

After thirty-five years as an MP, during which he held ministerial office only once (as junior minister for Northern Ireland from 1986–9), Viggers found perhaps his greatest fame by submitting a claim for a five-foot-high 'duck island' costing £1,645 to be paid out of Parliamentary expenses. He was then ordered to stand down as an MP by his party leader at the next general election. There is no more to be said. Duck off.

39

Bedlam by William Hogarth.

Robert Carteret

(1721–76) Yarmouth, Isle of Wight, 1744–7

Before the Parliamentary Reform Acts of 1832 and 1867 abolished corrupt electoral practices, many seats in the House of Commons were controlled by aristocrats simply for the benefit of their sons. Sometimes a peer's son was made an MP to give him something to do, with the Commons seen as a political nursery before assuming the responsibilities of a seat in the House of Lords. In the case of Robert Carteret, however, the Commons was his nursery in the fullest possible sense of the word, for he was completely mad.

His insanity was well known even before he was elected MP at the age of just twenty-three. Once, while a guest at Woburn Abbey, he suddenly woke his hosts, the Duke and Duchess of Bedford, at five in the morning, covered in blood. He held up his coat, and presented them with a great mass of horses' ears. A guest wrote: 'He had been in the [Duke's] stable and cropped all the horses.' According to another contemporary, Carteret was 'deficient in his intellects, fond of low company, profuse, fickle and debauched'. He spent most his time wandering aimlessly in St James's Park, dressed in the garment of a groom or a coachman.

Nevertheless, his father, Earl Granville, was determined that he should represent the family in the Commons, and he was elected for Yarmouth in 1744. There is no record of Carteret ever speaking in debates, and he seems to have figured out how to vote only once, in 1746. He stood down at the 1747 general election. He did manage to marry one Molly Paddock, 'a woman of vile extraction, bold, loose, and vulgar', but evidently did not succeed in working out the rest, for he died without issue in 1776, the last of his line.

Winston's Dad.

Lord Randolph Churchill

(1849–95) Conservative, Woodstock 1874–85,
South Paddington 1885–95

Churchill's career was one of those that promised much but delivered little. Despite being the architect of a new, populist form of Conservatism, which he called 'Tory Democracy', his main contribution to political history was his dramatic resignation.

From the outset of his political career in 1874 – the year when his son Winston was born – Churchill was seen as a rising star. But he had a knack of antagonizing the very people whose influence and support he needed. In 1875, he helped to save his brother from being named as co-respondent in Lord Aylesford's divorce case by threatening to publicize incriminating letters sent by one of Aylesford's friends to Lady Aylesford. Since that friend was the Prince of Wales, this was not, perhaps, the shrewdest move, and social ostracism beckoned for several years. He survived this, however, and began to build up his own power base within the Conservative Party.

His success in appealing to the grass roots made him a force to be reckoned with, although he never endeared himself to Sir Stafford Northcote, the leader of his party in the Commons. He openly undermined Northcote in opposition after 1880, with the creation of a party-within-a-party, the so-called 'Fourth Party'. However, this did not matter unduly, as Northcote was rapidly being eclipsed by the party leader in the Lords, the Marquis of Salisbury. Salisbury recognized Churchill's significance and made him Secretary of State for India and then Chancellor of the Exchequer (which he combined with the job of Leader of the Commons). But in 1886, Churchill threw away all his political advantage by attempting to bluff Salisbury. He threatened to resign in order to achieve cuts in defence. Salisbury called the bluff and let him go.

After his resignation, it seemed as if he might return, but no opportunity ever arose. Salisbury refused to offer him the Paris Embassy that he sought. Meanwhile, his health deteriorated. It was (and still is) widely suspected that he was suffering from secondary, and then tertiary, syphilis. Despite his son's subsequent denial of this diagnosis, Lord Randolph's behaviour became ever more erratic, and he died in 1895. We suspect that history might not have paid him much attention at all, had it not been for the achievements of his more successful son.

Tom Driberg, 1st Baron Bradwell

(1905–76) Independent & Labour, Maldon 1942–55, Barking 1959–74

Thomas Edward Neil Driberg had many attributes, but a devotion to Parliamentary duty was not among them. He spent most of his time working as a journalist and on his other main interest: blow jobs.

Elected first as an Independent, before taking the Labour whip, Driberg was an assiduous MP in his early Parliamentary career. However, from the 1950s onwards, he increasingly spent his time on writing and oral sex.

There can be few MPs whose skills in fellatio helped gain them a place in the *Dictionary of National Biography*, but, as the book states, 'Driberg had a consuming passion for fellating handsome, lean, intelligent working-class toughs.' Policemen, fellow politicians, miners and sailors were all among his conquests.

Driberg was also an effective, popular writer for newspapers and magazines, and preferred that to spending time on his work as an MP. When Clement Attlee's government was in its final days, calling in MPs from their sickbeds to help maintain their slim majority, Driberg was off for months at a time covering the Korean War. And we can be reasonably certain that his interest in military activity was not confined to the war effort. Men in uniform had often caught his attention. During the Second World War, he was once caught by a policeman when he was just about to service a sailor's 'long, uncircumcised, and tapering, but rock-hard erection'.

While that particular coitus ended in interruptus, most of his encounters were carried off successfully. Apart from one unsuccessful prosecution, Driberg was lucky. It was widely suspected that he had avoided exposure because he had so much incriminating material on pillars of the establishment. It is claimed that he performed fellatio on Nye Bevan, and that he even made a pass at Jim Callaghan. Despite his extracurricular activities, Driberg got married, to a Mrs Ena Mary Binfield. Upon the surprising event, one wag commented that 'she won't know which way to turn'.

Intelligent, cultured and able, Driberg might have made a good MP, but we think he deserves his place here for his constant distraction from Parliament. Unsurprisingly, although he was tolerated as an MP, he never achieved ministerial office – that, at least, his party might have found a little too hard to swallow.

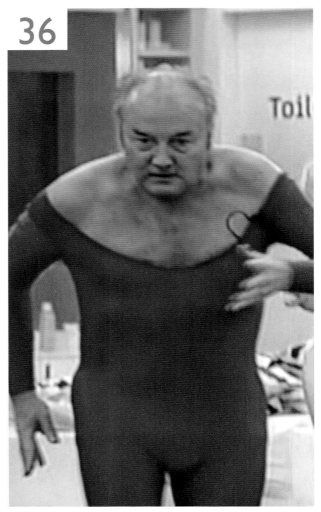

Big, brother.

George Galloway

(b.1954) Labour, Glasgow Hillhead 1987–97, Glasgow Kelvin 1997–2005, Respect, Bethnal Green & Bow, 2005–

George Galloway is very litigious. But we still think he is a crap MP.

Old Sarum, Wiltshire.

James Alexander

(1769–1848) Old Sarum 1812–32

£££

There may have been MPs in the unreformed days of Parliament who were more useless than James Alexander, but the accolade he receives here is not just for his own undoubted mediocrity. Uniquely, he is the only MP on this list who qualifies because of his constituency. Alexander was one of the last MPs for the seat of Old Sarum, the most glaring example of 'pocket boroughs' in the old electoral system before its reformation in 1832.

Old Sarum deserves its notorious reputation. Pocket boroughs were, literally, bought by wealthy proprietors, who were then able to make sure that the MPs were men who supported their interests. The Earl of Caledon bought Old Sarum in 1802. Just outside Salisbury, it was mostly a collection of old ditches and ramparts from a long-abandoned medieval settlement. In the borough, there were only three houses. You might think that living in the constituency would grant you the right to vote, but you would be wrong.

The Earl believed in 'one man, one vote' – just so long as that man was him. Attached to the borough were eleven 'burgages', which gave the holder the right to vote, and the Earl decided who held the burgages. These were granted to his friends and family, and in 1812, Caledon decided to elect his cousin, James Alexander, as one of the MPs. He knew the level of commitment he wanted from his Members, noting that if he decided to sell the borough, 'I am sure they would cheerfully resign.'

Alexander lived down to the Earl's expectations. He hardly ever spoke in Parliament, always voted with the government, supported the suspension of habeas corpus and defended the property tax. Caledon was so satisfied with his cousin that he exchanged estates with Alexander so that the MP took over the nominations. Unsurprisingly, he always elected himself. Although he has been justifiably forgotten by history, we feel that James Alexander deserves a special mention here: a crap MP for a crap constituency.

'PUNCH CANDIDATE for GUZZLEDOWN'

'Canvassing for Votes'.

Derek Conway

(b.1953) Conservative, Shrewsbury & Atcham 1983–97, Old Bexley & Sidcup 2001–

 £££

Imagine that you are one of Derek Conway's constituents. Plop onto the mat; Derek has sent you a Christmas card! And being from a senior Tory MP, it goes straight onto the mantelpiece. How nice of Derek to put his office staff on his Christmas card, you think. Perhaps he is thanking them for their hard work during the year. There's that nice Colette, his secretary. Then you remember Frederick whom you met once, and who Derek said was his researcher. And there's Henry next to him, apparently another researcher. You open the card: 'Merry Christmas from the Conways!'

Many MPs employ members of their family, but few as brazenly as Conway. The *Daily Telegraph* reported that tax-payers paid members of Conway's immediate family a total of more than £260,000 over a six-year period. However, it was found that Henry and Freddie were full-time students for some of the time they were employed, and the Commons Committee for Standards and Privileges began an investigation. In 2008, it concluded that Conway had 'overpaid his younger son, Freddie' and had 'awarded him excessive bonuses', despite the fact that he appeared to have been 'all but invisible during the period of his employment'. The sums involved were eye-watering. Young Freddie 'earned' up to £11,773 a year, plus bonuses, for almost three years. In total, he was paid £45,163 in gross salary, in addition to picking up pension contributions of about £4,500, which isn't bad considering he was meant to be studying geography at Newcastle University at the time. In 2009, the same committee found that Conway had also overpaid his son Henry. He was ordered to pay back thousands of pounds. Conway is standing down at the next election.

Peter Baker

(1921–66) Conservative, South Norfolk 1950–4

Peter Baker was expelled from Parliament in 1954. His crime, forgery, was not particularly heinous, and we mention him here only because we think it time for him to lose his distinction of being the last MP to be expelled from the House of Commons. Surely it is time for more?

Christopher Perne

(d.c.1566) Bossiney 1555, Plympton Erle 1558, St Ives 1559, Grampound 1563

Perne is proof that Parliament has always had its fair share of madmen, and even some kleptomaniacs. He first gained a seat in the Commons through his Protestant connections during the reign of Edward VI. But when Catholic Queen Mary came to the throne, he was involved in Henry Dudley's plot to replace her with her sister Princess Elizabeth, and was arrested and temporarily excluded from Parliament.

He was also excluded from the Royal Court, and told not to 'come near [it] by the space of seven miles, upon pain of forfeiture of £500'. This odd instruction may be connected to reports of Perne having taken up 'picking', or pickpocketing. In 1563, when still an MP, he was 'taken into a great mishap' and began to act in a 'lewd manner'. He was found stealing 'gold buttons', presumably from the clothing of wealthy colleagues, and was 'committed to the Marshalsea for pickery, without any notice given to the House'. Marshalsea Prison (later made famous by Charles Dickens) was not a nice place, and there Perne went mad. In 1566, he was declared a 'lunatick', and a new election writ was moved for his seat. There is no record of his death or later life.

Don't mention the war.

Nicholas Ridley

(1929–93) Conservative, Cirencester & Tewkesbury 1959–92

When, in 1972, the then Prime Minister Edward Heath decided to change the direction of his government's economic policy, he knew he would lose a number of ministers in protest. He was prepared to dismiss most of them, but seemingly calculated that the brilliant but abrasive Nicholas Ridley would be, to paraphrase Lyndon Johnson, better inside the tent pissing out, rather than the other way round. He offered Ridley the post of minister for the arts, but Ridley acidly declined the post, saying he did not believe the arts should even have a minister. Whether inside the tent or out, Ridley pissed on everyone; that was his style.

Although he was one of the most talented political thinkers of his generation, and an architect of a decade of Thatcherite economic policy, Ridley was often painfully unsuited to the demands of modern politics and the media age. This was mainly due to his unstinting inflexibility. He refused to believe in any opinion other than his own, and dismissed his critics with all the subtlety of Basil Fawlty. Once, during a BBC interview, he responded to a question by sneering, 'That is the most stupid question I've ever been asked.' When the interviewer bravely repeated the question, he replied, 'That is the second most stupid question I've ever been asked.' But the question was undoubtedly not as stupid as his answer to an interviewer on the subject of European integration in 1990; he claimed that it was 'all a German racket designed to take over the whole of Europe... I'm not against giving up sovereignty, but not to this lot. You might as well give it to Adolf Hitler, frankly.' The Germans were not amused, and Ridley had to resign as Secretary of State for Trade and Industry.

But gaffes aside, Ridley's intemperate nature led to serious miscalculations on matters of policy. He was right on many things, but also occasionally spectacularly wrong. For example, when at the Foreign Office during the early years of Thatcher's government, he advocated ceding sovereignty of the Falkland Islands to Argentina, against the wishes of the local residents, a decision which in part encouraged the Argentinean junta to believe that Britain would not fight for the Islands before they launched their invasion in 1982. Arguably, Ridley's greatest political blunder was his enthusiastic endorsement of the Poll Tax, about which he refused to tolerate objections. The tax was not his idea, but, as the Cabinet minister responsible, he wholeheartedly pushed for its immediate introduction. His phrase, 'Every time I hear people squeal, I am more than certain that we are right', seemed to sum up the Thatcher government's uncaring attitude.

Hazel Blears

(b.1956) Labour, Salford 1997–

£££ ➡️

Poor Hazel. She just wanted to be loved. And she was doing so well. After a series of junior ministerial positions, she joined the Cabinet in 2006 and quickly became one of the public faces of the government. If things were going badly, you could be certain that she would be touring the TV studios, and her chirpy voice would be on the *Today* programme to tell you just how rosy everything was in the garden. When she stood for the Labour deputy leadership in 2007, photos of her astride her motorbike showed her credentials as a woman of the people, while supporters' T-shirts proclaimed, 'We're Nuts About Hazel'. So popular had this bearer of good news become that, in the contest, she stormed to last place.

But nothing deterred the irrepressible Ms Blears. Nothing, that is, until the expenses scandal of 2009. No one would deny her commitment to her beloved Salford and its voters, but her attitude to other matters left her vulnerable to criticism. For tax purposes, she declared her London property her primary residence, which meant that she avoided capital gains tax on a hefty profit. But she had told the Commons' authorities that it was her second home – on which, of course, she could claim expenses. It turned out that she had stayed in expensive hotels for a while after she had sold her London home, and had then purchased a pricey bed and a new television. But who would begrudge her these little privileges?

When it turned out that lots of people did, she offered to pay back over £13,000 in capital gains tax and appeared on television brandishing the cheque. But that was not the end of the affair. In the *Observer*, Blears had unwisely chosen to deliver what most people regarded as criticism of a grisly internet performance by the Prime Minister: 'YouTube if you want to'. Gordon Brown returned the compliment, describing the way she had dealt with expenses as 'totally unacceptable behaviour'.

Unsurprisingly, her resignation followed shortly after, but it was one of the messiest recorded here. In June 2009, it was announced that she would be leaving at the next Cabinet reshuffle. The news was released on the eve of local and European elections, the campaign for which she had been partly responsible as Secretary of State for Communities and Local Government. She dressed for the occasion, wearing a brooch with the motto 'rocking the boat'. She later publicly regretted her actions, but was it too late to save her career? Only time will tell, but we're not nuts about Hazel.

Anthony Steen

(b.1939) Conservative, Liverpool Wavertree 1973–83, South Hams 1983–97, Totnes 1997–

£££

Anthony Steen was one of the more spectacular casualties of the 2009 expenses scandal. The *Daily Telegraph* reported that in one four-year period he claimed £87,729 for his second home, much of which was spent on his garden. The Parliamentary fees office made payments for a tree surgeon to inspect up to 500 trees, fencing to keep rabbits away from the shrubberies and the repair of a private sewage system. When Steen submitted one of the claims, a fees officer wrote on the bill, 'I've paid this, should I have?'

The public thought not, and there was an outcry. Steen tried vainly to protest his innocence, but he only made matters worse. His first defence was to suggest that the trees on his estate presented a health and safety risk to the public. When that failed to assuage voters' anger, he decided that attack was the best form of defence, and so took to the airwaves: 'I think I behaved, if I may say so, impeccably', he said. 'Do you know what it is about? Jealousy. I have got a very, very large house. Some people say it looks like Balmoral…It's not particularly attractive, it just does me nicely and it's got room to actually plant a few trees… I don't know what the fuss is about.' Steen placed all blame for the scandal on the 'wretched' Labour government, which had introduced the Freedom of Information Act used to publish details of MPs' expenses. He concluded, philosophically, 'What right does the public have to interfere with my private life? None. Do you know what this reminds me of? An episode of *Coronation Street*.' Steen announced that he would be standing down as MP at the next election. He had been an MP continuously since 1974. He has never been a minister. We wonder why.

27

Sir John Trevor

(c.1637–1717) Tory, Castle Rising 1673, Bere Alston 1679, Denbigh County 1681, Denbigh 1685, Bere Alston 1689, Yarmouth 1690

£££ 👢

Trevor was an accomplished lawyer and debater, and seemed destined for high office after entering the Commons in 1673. Initially, he had what you might call a safe seat, for he bought his own – the pocket borough of Castle Rising – for £60. He became Speaker in 1685 under James II, but fell from favour when William III became King in 1688. However, despite continued opposition from William, who considered him 'such a knave', Trevor was again elected Speaker in 1690. It is claimed that the practice of MPs standing up if they want to speak in the chamber, rather than simply staying seated to 'catch the Speaker's eye', began when Trevor was Speaker. He had such a bad squint that Members could never be sure who he was looking at.

In many respects Trevor was a good Speaker, but his period in office came to an abrupt end when it was found that he had accepted a bribe. The Common Council of London had given Trevor one thousand guineas (we hope in a brown envelope) to secure his support for the London Orphans Bill. Such bribes were common (indeed, pick the right Peer, and you can still do it today), but Trevor was caught because he asked for a receipt. He was found guilty by the House of 'high crime and misdemeanour', and removed from office in 1695. It seems that William III was a good judge of character after all.

SIR SAMUEL HOARE.

Sir Samuel Hoare,
Viscount Templewood

(1880–1959) Conservative, Chelsea 1910–44

Regardless of how one views those who 'appeased' Nazi Germany in the 1930s, Sir Samuel Hoare was one of the less appealing supporters of Neville Chamberlain's policies. Almost forgotten now, Hoare was a prim, ambitious, poor speaker who was also one of the pillars of the Conservative and National governments of the interwar years. However, Hoare was not a complete failure. He was an effective administrator who performed several of the most senior roles in government, including Secretary of State for India, Foreign Secretary, First Lord of the Admiralty and Home Secretary. Despite his generally unappealing personality, he might have escaped his inclusion here; but for one particular act, he deserves it.

In 1935, as Europe became more concerned about the policies of the dictators of Italy and Nazi Germany, the British government led by Stanley Baldwin seemed to take a firm line against aggression. The Italian dictator Mussolini looked likely to invade Abyssinia, but Foreign Secretary Hoare made a strong speech to the League of Nations. He made clear British support for collective resistance. When the government won an election later that year, one of the main planks of its manifesto was support for the League of Nations. But Mussolini ignored all the warnings and invaded Abyssinia anyway. Hoare was about to go off on holiday but was persuaded to stop off in Paris for a meeting with his opposite number, Pierre Laval, to coordinate a response to the invasion. And what was their cunning plan? To hand over most of Abyssinia to Mussolini, in the Hoare–Laval Pact.

Hoare went off skating in Switzerland, where he fell over and injured himself. To add insult to injury, he returned to find that the country was in uproar over the treatment of Abyssinia. Although the Cabinet had originally supported him, it abandoned him as quickly as he had abandoned Abyssinia, and he resigned. When he saw George V, the King reportedly joked, 'No more coals to Newcastle, no more Hoares to Paris.' Hoare did not see the funny side.

Although Hoare was brought back soon enough, his career never really recovered. Churchill, who had long disliked him, dismissed him from the Cabinet in 1940, and eventually he was sent to be ambassador to Spain, where it was thought he could cause the least difficulty. It was feared by some that he might collaborate if Britain were to be invaded. But he was a successful ambassador, and later wrote well-received memoirs. He was luckier than Pierre Laval, who joined the wartime Vichy government. After the war, he was taken out and shot.

Horatio Bottomley, M.P.
South Hackney.

J. Benjamin Stone
1911

Horatio Bottomley

(1860–1933) Independent,
Hackney South 1906–12, 1918–22

£££ ||||

Politicians and fraudsters often excel at the same disciplines. The skills of persuasion and advocacy needed to make people give you their vote are precisely those needed to make people give you their money. A large number of fraudsters have therefore found it surprisingly easy to become MPs. Robert Maxwell is a modern example, but in the early twentieth century none was more famous than Horatio Bottomley.

Bottomley was always interested in politics, and began his career as a publisher. His first paper was reasonably successful, and he found an ingenious way of increasing profits by taking bribes from politicians in return for favourable publicity. He quickly found that he was proficient at separating the gullible from their money, mainly through a combination of his own persuasiveness and engineering third-party endorsements. He somehow managed to become a board member of the *Financial Times*, which reported that he was 'a man of millions'. By 1900 he had made a fortune through a series of investment schemes, mostly fraudulent, built on the craze for mining and gold.

For Bottomley, there was no greater endorsement than the appellation 'MP'. He was an excellent orator, and in 1906, after several false starts, he won an election for Hackney South. His dishonest reputation preceded him in the Commons, and his maiden speech was heard in disdainful silence. But he found that wit won him friends, and he grudgingly earned his colleagues' attention through humour, referring to himself, for example, as a 'more-or-less honourable Member'.

By 1912, however, his various frauds began to unravel, and he was declared bankrupt and expelled from the Commons. Undeterred, he decided to start again, and founded another newspaper, *The John Bull*, a radical nationalist paper that was wildly successful, thanks, in part, to the outbreak of the Great War. Bottomley's patriotic fervour, calling for the extermination of all 'Germ-huns' in Britain and for Germany to be 'wiped off the map of Europe', went down well, and after the war, Bottomley, despite his numerous exposed frauds, found himself back in Parliament in 1918. But he could not resist another swindle. He exploited the national mood by launching the 'Victory Bond Club'. It was another failure, and in 1922 he was convicted of fraud, expelled from the Commons and sentenced to seven years in jail. A story exists that one day the prison chaplain at Wormwood Scrubs found Bottomley mending mail bags. 'Sewing Bottomley?', he asked. 'No, reaping', came the answer.

Fletcher Norton, 1st Baron Grantley

(1716–89) Appleby 1756–61,
Wigan 1761–8, Guildford 1768–82

£££

When Michael Martin (no. 19) resigned as Speaker in June 2009, it was widely reported that he was the first Speaker to be forced out of office since Sir John Trevor (no. 27) in 1695. That is true only in so far as Martin and Trevor resigned their office, for Fletcher Norton, too, was effectively forced out as well. He had every intention of remaining as Speaker in 1780, but was defeated in a vote of the House after he had systematically offended both the government and opposition, as well as the King.

Norton began his career as a barrister, where he earned a reputation (which followed him to the Commons) for corruption. He was alleged to have taken money from both sides of cases he was involved in, and since he looked like a bulldog, he gained the unfortunate nickname of Sir Bull-Face Double-Fee. At first his forthrightness worked to his advantage. He once accused Pitt the Elder of inciting rebellion, claiming that Pitt 'chilled my blood'. Pitt responded by challenging Norton to a duel, saying, 'I shall be glad to meet him in any place…when his blood is warmer.' Pitt's opponents liked such exchanges, and Norton was elected Speaker in 1770.

But the Speaker's chair gave Norton the confidence to be even more insulting, when his position called for at least an appearance of impartiality. On one occasion he swore loudly at the Prime Minister, Lord North, alleging that North had reneged on a promise to give him the well-paid post of Chief Justice of the Common Pleas.

His biggest mistake, however, was to insult King George III, which was unwise in an age when the monarch still exercised considerable control in Parliament. When George asked the Commons for an increase in the civil list, Norton announced that the King already had money 'great beyond your Majesty's wants', and should spend what he had more 'wisely'. Finally, in 1780, Norton further insulted the King by openly supporting John Dunning's famous motion: 'The influence of the Crown has increased, is increasing, and ought to be diminished.' That same year a rival candidate for Speaker, Thomas Townshend, was quickly found to replace Norton on the grounds of his 'ill health'. Norton protested that he felt well enough, but was nonetheless defeated. He was given a peerage in consolation, thus establishing the precedent that retiring Speakers, even bad ones, are sent to the Lords.

Mad Jack.

John Fuller

(1757–1834) Southampton 1780–4, Sussex 1801–12

'Mad Jack' Fuller ranks among the nineteenth century's most useless MPs. He joined no party and sat in Parliament chiefly to defend his own interests. Since these mostly involved the protection of his sugar plantations in Jamaica, he is best remembered as a proud supporter of slavery. In one such debate he claimed that the condition of slaves in the West Indies was better than that of the working classes in England.

It was thanks to the likes of Fuller that William Wilberforce's attempts to abolish the slave trade took twenty years, only succeeding in 1807. Supporters of slavery regularly filled Commons' committees with suppliers of false evidence, suggesting, for example, that captured slaves rejoiced at the opportunity to work in the West Indies and lived in huts fumigated with lime and lavender.

Fuller was also a drunk, and he repeatedly scandalized the Commons with his intoxicated outbursts and ridiculous interventions. Once, during a debate on the Walcheren expedition, Fuller heckled Prime Minister William Pitt so much that Fuller had to be overpowered by the Serjeant and four messengers, who bundled him out of the chamber. Fuller particularly disliked the Speaker, whom he called 'the insignificant little fellow in the wig', and on another occasion, having 'entered the House in a state of inebriety, too audibly mistook the Speaker for an owl in an ivy-bush'. John Fuller was educated at Eton.

Long live King Francis II!

Sir William Blackett, 2nd Baronet

(1690–1728) Tory, Newcastle-upon-Tyne 1710–28

In 1688 William of Orange invaded England and deposed the Catholic King, James II. The defining political divide of the late seventeenth and early eighteenth centuries therefore fell between the 'Tories', who generally supported the exiled monarch, and the 'Whigs', those who supported the new Protestant regime of William (and his successor Queen Anne). The Tory/Whig split formed the origin of modern party politics in Britain. MPs of the time were often in an impossible position. Should they support the return of James II and his heirs (the 'Jacobites'), whom they viewed to be the rightful kings, or keep quiet and hope not to lose their wealth and influence? Like many nominal Tories, Sir William Blackett decided to hedge his bets, and see which way the political wind would blow.

For years the Whigs were in the ascendancy. However, a crisis came when Queen Anne died in 1714. Because she had no heir, and because those next in line to the throne were all Catholics, the Whigs, desperate to ensure a Protestant succession, had passed the Act of Settlement, banning all Catholics from succeeding to the throne. As a result, the Protestant George of Hanover was invited to take the Crown. Dozens of candidates with a superior claim to the throne were excluded because they were Catholics. The Hanoverian succession, and the succession of all monarchs ever since, was either a celebration of British Parliamentary liberty, or a hypocrisy born of prejudice, depending on your view. In 1715 the son of James II, the 'Pretender' James III, launched a rebellion, sensing disaffection with Britain's new German monarch, George I.

One of those James believed would support him was Sir William Blackett, a Tory from Northumberland. Blackett was among those charged with seizing control of Newcastle to await an invading army from Scotland, and had organized and armed a large number of workers from his estate. At the last moment, however, he changed his mind, and failed to rebel. The Whigs issued a warrant for his arrest, and he 'was much pursued by the King's forces, who suspected him to be in the rebels interest'. He fled to London to protest his loyalty and, like many of his fellow Tories, sought the earliest opportunity 'to kiss the King's hand'. Newcastle remained loyal to George I, the rebellion collapsed and James III fled to exile.

It is still illegal for a Catholic to become monarch. A lineal descent of those excluded from the throne by the Whigs still exists, though, and today, the Jacobite 'successor' to the English and Scottish thrones is Francis, Duke of Bavaria. Were the Act of Settlement ever to be repealed, he would arguably be King. In which case, we would simply exchange one German family for another.

Asleep on the job.

Antony, Lord Lambton

(1922–2006) Conservative,
Berwick-upon-Tweed 1951–73

In many ways, Lord Lambton is unfortunate to have ended up here. We have no desire to impugn his abilities as a constituency member, and he was an able and popular minister. But he was, by his own admission, also very foolish, and for that he earns his place.

Antony Claud Frederick Lambton, known as Viscount Lambton, was the son of the 5th Earl of Durham, disclaiming the title in 1970 in order to remain in the House of Commons as a Conservative MP. In the Heath government of 1970, Lambton was made a junior defence minister. So far, so ordinary. But Lambton liked to relax with a prostitute in Maida Vale named Norma Russell, and he was very careless how he went about it – even paying her with his own cheques.

All might perhaps have been well had she not got married. Her new husband, Colin Levy, revealed to police that Lambton was her customer, and suggested that he was involved in drugs. In a bizarre incident, Levy then sought evidence for the newspapers via a microphone hidden in the nose of a cuddly toy. Secret photographs were taken, and eventually Levy sold the story to the *Sunday People*, which passed it on to police.

News of these events reached the Prime Minister – whom we must assume had limited knowledge of prostitutes in Maida Vale – and Lambton promptly resigned.

He was also prosecuted for possession of cannabis and barbiturates, although he claimed the former had been confiscated from a friend and the latter were for medicinal purposes. All in all, the incident was pretty small beer, and we suspect that, if it happened now, it would be overlooked. He was unlucky, but, as he himself put it: 'I behaved with incredible stupidity.'

41

'I tend to be a lone voice ploughing a lonely field'

Terry Dicks

(b. 1937) Conservative, Hayes & Harlington 1983–97

Terry Dicks seems to have been one of the Labour Party's least favourite Tory MPs after Mrs Thatcher. Although that alone does not qualify him for inclusion here, his unorthodox views on everything from performing artists (or 'arty-farty people pushing themselves around the Royal Opera House'), to HIV sufferers ('AIDS', he once declared, 'is a self-inflicted luvvies illness') certainly do. The late Tony Banks MP described him as 'living proof that a pig's bladder on a stick can get elected to Parliament'.

Dicks often appeared to epitomize the worst stereotypes of Conservative MPs in the late 1980s and 1990s. He was seemingly unmoved when HIV/Aids first came to public prominence; he branded the government's educational efforts on the disease as 'a completely unnecessary publicity campaign which helps no one and which will make no difference'.

At the height of public hysteria over the disease he called for every health worker to undergo mandatory HIV testing, and labelled the Terrence Higgins Trust a 'luvvies charity for the AIDS people'.

Dicks lost his seat in 1997. His successor, John McDonnell, paid tribute to his efforts as an MP in his maiden speech. 'Despite my respect for the conventions of the House, I shall not perjure myself by praising my immediate Tory predecessor. Many saw him simply as a Tory buffoon…When he chose as his election slogan, "We love Dicks", we were not sure whether to laugh or to call in the obscene publications squad.

'However, Terry Dicks was not a joke. He was a stain on the character of this House, the Conservative Party which harboured him and the good name of my constituency. He brought shame on the political process of this country by his blatant espousal of racism and his various corrupt dealings. He demeaned the House by his presence, and I deeply regret that the Conservative Party failed to take action to stem his flow of vile bigotry. Thankfully, my constituents can now say good riddance to this malignant creature.' Although we are in no position to confirm the veracity of McDonnell's allegations, and should point out that we have found little evidence to support them, we cannot say that we love Dicks too.

Kerr-ching!

Michael Martin

(b.1945) Labour, Glasgow Springburn 1979–2005,
Glasgow North East 2005–9

It is said that Michael Martin, Speaker of the House of Commons from 2000 to 2009, is sensitive to public criticism, so he may be perturbed to find himself listed here. And not for one moment do we suggest he was anything less than diligent as MP for his Glasgow constituency. But, given his distinction of being the first Speaker forced to resign since Sir John Trevor (no. 27), he cannot escape inclusion.

An initial lack of warmth for Martin in some quarters was perhaps rather unfair. There was a misplaced belief that convention had been breached when Martin, a Labour MP, succeeded Betty Boothroyd, another Labour MP. But it is difficult to see how the election of his main rival would have been more widely welcomed; Sir George Young was the man who had presided over the deeply unpopular privatization of British Rail, a decision which many will rue long after Michael Martin has been forgotten. Martin's subsequent unpopularity in the House, however, was all his own doing.

Despite grumbles over his chairing of debates, he had been Speaker for eight years before things really started to go wrong. In 2008, his own spokesman was forced to resign after he had unintentionally misled the press about the (rather large) taxi expenses of Martin's wife. Then, later the same year, Martin was embroiled in the controversial case of the Conservative spokesman Damian Green, arrested and questioned by the police over allegations about Whitehall leaks. The police were allowed to search Green's office without a warrant, the permission for which Martin was ultimately responsible, and which triggered widespread outrage.

But the time bomb ticking away in the background for Martin, as for so many, was the question of MPs' expenses. Martin and the Commons' authorities had resisted the publication of expenses for a long period. When the scale of the abuse of the system became clear, and public anger rose, more and more questions were asked about Martin's role, and whether he was the right man to preside over the disinfecting of the system. Everything came to a head with a truly execrable performance in the Commons in May 2009, when Martin faced successive points of order from all sides of the House requesting his resignation. Apparently bewildered and even uncertain about the procedure of the House, he refused to answer the points directly. It was a sorry sight, and even Martin realized the game was up, resigning the following day. It is said that Martin's critics resented a former sheet-metal worker becoming Speaker. We fear the real reason was they thought he wasn't much good.

John Story

(c.1503–71) MP for Salisbury, Hindon, East Grinstead, Bramer, Bath, Ludgershall and Downton 1545–59

John Story represents an extreme example of the difficulties faced by MPs during the English Reformation, as the religious pendulum swung from Protestantism to Catholicism and back again. Story was an ardent Catholic, and owed his seat purely to the intervention of Catholic bishops, whose Parliamentary attack dog he became.

Story's career began badly. In 1549, he became the first MP to be imprisoned and expelled by the Commons, for his comment, 'Woe unto thee England when the king is a child' (Edward VI was eleven). But when the Catholic Queen Mary succeeded Edward VI in 1553, Story re-entered the Commons and used his position to persecute Protestant 'hereticks' with vigour. His most notable victim was Thomas Cranmer, Archbishop of Canterbury. Story believed that the best way to restore Catholicism to England was through violence: what he called 'the sharpness of the sword'. He created an iron cage for roasting heretics alive, whipped anyone found carrying an English Bible and claimed to have been involved in over three hundred burnings. It was even rumoured that he had consigned his own relatives to the flames.

Unsurprisingly, Story fled England soon after the accession of the Protestant Elizabeth I. But such was the notoriety of this 'impudent papist', who had 'most traitorously meant the destruction of our dear and sovereign lady, Queen Elizabeth', that he was kidnapped and brought back to London, where he was hung, drawn and quartered at Tyburn.

Witnesses recalled that he 'did not only roare and cry like a hellhound, but also strake the executioner doing his office, and resisted as long as strength did serve him, beinge kept downe by three or foure men, until he was deade'. Catholics remember him more fondly, and he was beatified in 1886.

Frederick North, 2nd Earl of Guilford, 'Lord North'

(1732–92) Tory, Banbury, 1754–90

It all seemed to be going so well. North, appointed in 1770 as the youngest Prime Minister yet, was feted in the Commons, beloved by King George III and destined for a sustained period in office as glorious as that of Sir Robert Walpole. Yet he resigned in disgrace in 1782. North was 'the Man who Lost America'.

Even before the Americans began their rebellion, there were ominous signs that North was unsuited to the task of holding together Britain's disparate empire. He was, in modern political language, a hardliner, and refused to tolerate any diminution of the Crown's power. He had earlier led the government's attacks against John Wilkes, the libertarian and advocate of free speech, and he had consistently advocated authoritarian measures in America, such as the infamous Stamp Act derided by the Colonists as 'taxation without representation'.

When news of the Boston 'tea party' reached London in 1773, North miscalculated, deciding that coercion was needed. His measures, including the Boston Port Act, merely exacerbated the situation, and outright war became inevitable. Although North was not solely to blame, the government's handling of the war was disastrous, and as defeat followed defeat, he tried repeatedly to resign. In 1778, he wrote to the King (in the third person, as etiquette dictated) that 'the anxiety of his mind has deprived Lord North of his memory and understanding'.

He later pleaded with George III to make Pitt the Elder Prime Minister in his place, but Pitt dropped dead in the House of Lords one week later. North belatedly tried to offer concessions to the Americans, but by then it was too late. When he heard of the decisive British surrender at Yorktown in 1781, he said, 'Oh God! It is all over.' He was right, and after a bruising censure debate in the Commons, he was supported by just nineteen MPs. He was finally able to resign, and with him, in an important precedent, went his entire ministry.

'... So barbarously executed, that he was cut down alive, and saw his bowels thrown into the fire.'

Thomas Harrison

(1616–60) Wendover 1646, 'Barebones' Parliament 1653

No other MP, save perhaps Oliver Cromwell, has tried so hard to abolish the House of Commons than Thomas Harrison. Unlike Cromwell, however, Harrison wanted to abolish the Commons not to extend his own power, but to extend the power of God.

Harrison was a Fifth Monarchist, a group of fanatics who believed that the year 1666, because it was reminiscent of the devil's number 666, was the year in which Christ would return to earth and rule with an army of saints. Their main enemy was the Pope, whom they saw as the antichrist. Fifth Monarchists sought to prepare the world for Christ's arrival by overthrowing the existing political and social order on earth, preferably by violence. Naturally, this involved the execution of Charles I, and Harrison emerged as a leader of the 'Fifth Monarchy Men' not just because he had fought in the Civil War and signed Charles I's death warrant, but also because he particularly liked killing Catholics. He once shot a Catholic officer who had surrendered, saying 'cursed is he that doeth the work of the Lord negligently'.

During the Protectorate, Harrison urged Cromwell to abolish the House of Commons and replace it with a chamber of religious guardians, on one occasion storming the Commons with troops and pulling the venerable Speaker Lenthall from his chair. Sadly, Harrison did not live to see the return of Christ in 1666, for on Charles II's restoration in 1660, he was immediately arrested as a threat to the nation.

As a Regicide he was sentenced to death by hanging, drawing and quartering, which he underwent, according to the watching Samuel Pepys, 'as cheerfully as any man could in that condition… the first blood shed in revenge for the blood of the King'. Like others in this list, Harrison believed that he was accountable only to God for his actions. But, as his violent death demonstrates, religious accountability and political accountability do not always mix well.

Red Ron.

Ron Brown

(1940–2007) Labour Edinburgh Leith 1979–92

It is difficult to know where to start with 'Red Ron'. Indeed, it is difficult to know how he managed to fit his Parliamentary duties in between his many other antics. Early on in his career, the left-wing Labour MP attracted attention by posing with

Soviet tanks after they had invaded Afghanistan, then flew to meet Colonel Gaddafi in 1984, not long after WPC Yvonne Fletcher had been shot near the Libyan Embassy in London.

He was suspended several times from the House of Commons for breaches of Parliamentary etiquette. Most notoriously, in a 1988 debate over the Poll Tax, Brown 'did a Heseltine' by grabbing the Commons mace and waving it around, but then he dropped it. When called to apologize by the Speaker, he repeatedly failed to do so, although he had already agreed that he would. For this, he was suspended again and had the party whip temporarily withdrawn. Later, when a private prosecution was attempted for his damage to the mace, he allegedly punched the man delivering the summons.

Just a month later came the next allegation, by another Labour MP, that Brown had been cavorting with a woman in the Commons shower. 'The only thing that was visible', recounted Bill O'Brien MP, 'was his mace.' But Brown denied the allegation about his activities with Nonna Longden, the woman in question. In January 1990, however, he was accused of damaging Longden's flat, and of theft. The police had found him in possession of some jewellery – and two pairs of knickers. Brown admitted that he and Longden had been lovers. He was acquitted of theft, but convicted of criminal damage – apparently caused in his anger at her new lover. Shortly after, he was deselected by his local party. In 1992, he stood as an Independent candidate, and lost heavily.

The Commons was a more boring place without Red Ron, but we bow to the views of his constituents and his party; he is worthy of his place here.

Rt Hon John Aislabie

(1670–1742) Tory & Whig, Ripon 1695–1702,
Northallerton 1702–5, Ripon 1705–21

⬤ £££ ||||

From the fourteenth century onwards, the House of Commons'
most important role was raising taxes for the Crown. The
Crown spent the money, and invariably asked for more. The
Commons, as the representative body of the people who paid
the taxes, therefore acted as a brake on the Crown (and thus
the government) from spending too much money. Over time,
however, the Crown and Commons fought for supremacy, and by
the end of the seventeenth century the Commons had effectively
won, meaning that the government now generally sat within

the Commons, and thereby controlled it. Thus, one of the reasons we pay so much tax today is because there is no longer a separate body able to restrain the government's spending.

In the eighteenth century, however, this situation was exacerbated by corruption. Those MPs who were senior members of the government often found that their ability to raise taxes, and their control of the money, meant that it was almost impossible to resist stealing it. One of the most corrupt such men (always men) was John Aislabie, who was Chancellor of the Exchequer from 1718 to 1721.

As Chancellor, Aislabie proposed a cunning plan to effectively eliminate the national debt by transferring it to the South Sea Company, a trading business which, despite engaging in a spot of slavery, was really a form of bank. The Company's shareholders had already grown rich from taking on earlier government debts in return for a fixed and perpetual annuity from the government, and the share price had risen dramatically.

But in 1720, with the prospect of acquiring even more debt at attractive rates, the share price rose exponentially, giving rise to the famous 'South Sea Bubble'. Aislabie's plan was passed by the House, and all was well until the bubble collapsed. Thousands of people were left destitute. It was soon found that Aislabie had not only taken a massive bribe from the Company to get the debt plan enacted, but had himself speculated heavily in the shares. He tried desperately to burn any incriminating evidence, but an inquiry concluded that he had instigated a 'most notorious, infamous, and dangerous corruption'. He was expelled from the Commons, sent to the Tower and barred from holding any office again. He did, however, manage to keep most of his money, much of which he spent (like many of today's MPs) on his garden at Studley Royal, in Yorkshire. You can visit it today, price: £8.25.

13

Tim Smith

(b.1947) Conservative, Ashfield 1974–9,
Beaconsfield 1982–97

£££ ➡

Tim Smith was an otherwise anonymous Conservative MP who
performed a series of worthy but junior roles, ending up as a
minister at the Northern Ireland Office. Had it not been for

his novel use of office stationery, his claim on the attention of political historians would have been limited. His sole achievement would probably have been the defeat of one A.C.L. Blair in the Beaconsfield by-election in 1982, which had delayed by a few months the Parliamentary arrival of Labour's next Prime Minister.

But, like many Tory MPs of the 1980s, Smith was keen on personal entrepreneurship. However, he took this interest further than most. He was in touch with a political lobbyist who included among his clients the businessman Mohammed al-Fayed. Al-Fayed was allegedly told that 'you need to rent an MP like you rent a London taxi'. In his high-profile dispute with Lonhro owner 'Tiny' Rowland, who had been angered by the Egyptian's purchase of House of Fraser, al-Fayed sought the support of Conservative MPs.

Along with a number of others, Smith worked hard on al-Fayed's behalf. Smith's constituents might reasonably have asked why he was spending valuable Parliamentary time on the interests of a wealthy foreign businessman. But, if they knew of his interest in al-Fayed's affairs, perhaps they put it down to a generous spirit. However, it was al-Fayed's generosity, rather than Smith's, that ensured his case was pressed so vigorously. In return for asking his questions, Smith received payments from al-Fayed, delivered in paper envelopes like a cash-in-hand payment to a plumber.

In 1994, after the failure of al-Fayed's appeal against the DTI report into his takeover of House of Fraser, information about the matter reached the *Guardian*, who accused Smith of taking 'cash-for-questions' in October 1994. Smith immediately admitted that the allegations were true and resigned from his ministerial job. He stood down as an MP in 1997, having immortalized the brown paper envelope in British political history.

'A dissolute and wasteful manner of life'.

William Parry

(d.1585) Queenborough, 1584

William Parry, a Welshman, was the only MP of the late sixteenth century to be arrested for treason. Although he was an MP for just a year, he still ranks as one of the most inept Members in Parliamentary history. A desire for money seems to have been the cause of Parry's downfall. He was perpetually in debt, despite marrying two rich widows (whom he ruined, and slept with their daughters), and devised a series of extraordinary schemes to find his fortune.

In the sixteenth century the quickest way to make money was to ingratiate yourself at the Royal Court, where service might secure a governmental post or pension. Parry, therefore, decided to attach himself to the service of Lord Burghley, and volunteered as a spy. By acting as a double agent, he successfully 'uncovered' a Catholic plot to assassinate Queen Elizabeth I, and for this he was rewarded with a seat in Parliament. But feeling that he had not received enough to clear his debts, he decided to repeat the trick, and tried to uncover another 'plot'.

This time, however, he took matters too far. Parry pretended to a known Catholic, Edmund Neville, that he himself was willing to assassinate Elizabeth, in the hope of inducing Neville to confess a rebellious intent. Then, instead of raising attention to the alleged plot through the usual channels, Parry decided to raise the matter directly with the Queen, in the hope of winning her royal gratitude, and money.

He tried to catch the Queen's attention with a speech in the House of Commons in which he hinted at a deadly threat against her, but refused to reveal any details unless he could tell the Queen directly. But the speech was so disastrous, Parry was placed under arrest for contempt, and never got to see Elizabeth. And within weeks of him publicizing the alleged plot, Edmund Neville predictably revealed that, in fact, it had been Parry himself who had suggested assassinating the Queen. Parry was immediately taken to the Tower and, bizarrely, promptly confessed, no doubt hoping for a pardon. But it was too late, and he was sentenced to death. The House of Commons petitioned the Queen that some of form of execution even more painful than the traditional hanging, drawing and quartering be devised for 'that villainous traitor Parry', and the execution was carried out barbarously. One witnessed recalled that 'when his bowelles were taken out, he gave a great groane'.

'the Champion Hypocrite of England'.

Jabez Spencer Balfour

(1843–1916) Liberal, Tamworth 1880–5, Burnley 1889–92

£££

Jabez Balfour was the most celebrated fraudster of his age, and was known as 'the Champion Hypocrite of England'. In the nineteenth century, when there was, in effect, no such thing as financial regulation, it was incredibly easy to establish investment frauds and pyramid schemes. But Balfour's uniquely vicious plan was to target the relatively poor yet growing lower middle classes by tapping into the late Victorian obsession for self-improvement, worthiness and piety. He presented himself as a champion of the temperance (or teetotal) movement, and launched the 'Liberator Building Society' in 1868.

The Society promised both attractive rates of return and the chance to 'liberate' the industrious poor by providing them with the means to buy their own home. Balfour was feted as a moral champion of the day. But in fact, the Society was merely a front behind which Balfour, through false accounts, lies and deception, was actually buying property from himself at inflated prices. The scam worked only as long as people continued to believe in Balfour and invest in the 'Liberator', and so, like Bernie Madoff with his ostentatious support of charities, Balfour sought to enter Parliament as a way of burnishing his trustworthiness. He became MP for Tamworth, the famous seat of Sir Robert Peel, in 1880.

Balfour was able to maintain the fraud as long as the general economy continued to grow. But the recession of the early 1890s led to a collapse in property prices, and the inevitable fall of his business. He resigned his seat in 1892 and fled to Argentina, leaving behind the thousands of investors who lost everything, a number of whom killed themselves.

Blair Babe.

Margaret Moran

(b.1955) Labour, Luton South 1997–

£££

It is hard to see which part of 'wholly, exclusively and necessarily incurred for the performance of a Member's parliamentary duties' Margaret Moran never completely understood. The seemingly self-serving nature of her interpretation of the rules governing Parliamentary expenses reminds us of those MPs of the eighteenth and nineteenth centuries who viewed a parliamentary seat as little more than a platform for self-enrichment. Moran, who was often among the top claimers during her brief, inglorious career, came to symbolize the failure of the expenses system, most particularly the 'Additional Costs Allowance' by which MPs could nominate any property they wished as their 'second home' for expenses claims.

The *Daily Telegraph*'s investigation into Moran's expenses claims revealed that in one four-year period she spent almost £8,000 on a new kitchen, carpets and a bed at her first designated second home in Westminster, then over £10,000 for gardening work, bathroom repairs, bedding, food, various items of DIY equipment, a stereo system and decorators' fees at her second designated second home in her constituency of Luton South and, finally, claimed £22,500 to treat dry rot at her third designated second home in Southampton, which was not only one hundred miles from her constituency but had belonged to her partner, Mick.

At first, Moran tried to claim that it was legitimate for the taxpayer to fund her partner's dry-rot repairs, because she could not effectively serve her constituents without his full support.

This was a strange defence, and one which, oddly enough, was not used by Jacqui Smith when it emerged that the taxpayer had been funding her husband's porn films. Moran later agreed to repay the £22,500 but never apologized, saying only that she understood her 'constituents' anger at the current fees regime'.

The dry-rot treatment was not Moran's only questionable use of Parliamentary resources. Perhaps the most damning indictment of her claims was the example shown by her colleague, Luton North MP Kelvin Hopkins; he never claimed for a second home, choosing to live solely in his constituency (indeed, on the same street as Moran) and commuted to Westminster every day by train. Moran's claims were eventually referred to a disciplinary committee, and she was barred by the Labour Party from standing as a Labour MP at the next election.

E.H.VERNEY

Edmund Hope Verney

(1838–1910) Liberal, North Buckinghamshire
1885–6, 1889–91

We can't quite believe it, but Edmund Hope Verney seems to have been the only MP expelled from the Commons for sexual deviancy. His fall is particularly noteworthy, for like so many MPs caught with their trousers down, he had publicly advocated the strictest standards of morality.

As a decorated veteran of the Crimean War and the Indian Mutiny, as well as a future baronet, Verney was able to present himself as an impeccably upstanding member of society. His wife, Margaret, was a diligent social campaigner, and he prided himself on collecting early editions of the Bible, which he listed as a recreation in *Who's Who*. He was elected to the Commons in 1885 as a Gladstonian Liberal, following his leader's pious tone, especially on foreign policy, where he steadily attacked the imperialist policies of the Conservatives. It came as something of a shock to his colleagues, therefore, to discover that he had pleaded guilty at the Old Bailey to 'unlawfully inciting and procuring Eugenie Rouillier to procure Nellie Maud Baskett, to have carnal connection with him', not least because the poor Miss Baskett was distinctly underage. Verney was sentenced to twelve months in prison, and promptly expelled from Parliament. His fellow MPs seem to have been anxious to avoid association with the worst aspect of his crime, for the record states only that Miss Baskett was procured for 'an immoral purpose'.

The Rt Hon Andrew Mackay & Julie Kirkbride

(b.1949) & (b.1960) Conservative, Birmingham Stechford 1977–9, East Berkshire 1983–97, Bracknell 1997– & Conservative, Bromsgrove 1997–

£££ ➡ 📷

A double entry for husband and wife MPs Andrew Mackay and Julie Kirkbride, who married in 1997. We happily acknowledge that both were in many ways excellent constituency MPs. However, the circumstances and manner of their Parliamentary departure demonstrated a gross misreading of the public mood at the height of the 2009 expenses scandal.

Both came unstuck over the issue of their second home. MPs are entitled to claim an allowance for their second home, which is generally either in their constituency or in London. The theory is that they pay for their 'main' home, like everybody else, but taxpayers pay for their additional home. Because Mackay and Kirkbride were married, however, Mackay was able to register his main home as a property in Worcestershire on which his wife was claiming her second home allowance, while she listed her main home as a property in London on which he was claiming his second home allowance. Mackay arguably had no 'main' home at all. His constituents were surprised to find that he didn't have a home in his constituency. 'It was all approved', he said, 'and frankly until it was drawn to my attention, it did not occur to me that it didn't pass the reasonableness test. Looking back now, it does look strange…' When the news broke, Mackay promptly resigned as David Cameron's Parliamentary adviser.

There it might have ended, but for the incompetent manner in which both Mackay and Kirkbride attempted to rescue their political careers. Mackay's chances were doomed from the moment he faced a private gathering of angry constituents in Bracknell, and claimed to the waiting media outside that he had received 'applause from around three-quarters of the audience, while around a quarter were critics'. Those emerging from the meeting watched in disbelief as he gave the interview, and, on live TV, immediately contradicted him. Later, film emerged of his constituents' furious outbursts. One even called him a 'thieving toad'.

Attention inevitably then focused on Kirkbride. It was alleged that her brother had been living rent-free in her taxpayer-funded second home. Perhaps the final blow came when the press printed a series of photographs of Kirkbride posing provocatively in a cornfield – these photos had also apparently been claimed on expenses, at a cost of £1,040. Both Mackay and Kirkbride have announced that they will be standing down at the next election.

7

Rt Hon John Thomson Stonehouse

(1925–88) Labour, Wednesbury 1957–74,
Walsall North 1974–6

£££ ◌◌

On 21 November 1974, after a pile of clothes was found on a Miami beach, the Labour MP and former minister John Stonehouse was declared missing, presumed dead. Obituaries were written, the House of Commons held a minute's silence and his grieving wife began preparations for a body-less funeral. It was believed that he had been eaten by a shark.

Five weeks later, however, Stonehouse was found alive in Australia, having been arrested for using a false passport by police on the hunt for Lord Lucan. Mrs Stonehouse was delighted, and flew out to Australia for an emotional reunion. But Stonehouse's elaborate defence of suffering a mental breakdown soon began to unravel. In an extreme example of constituency casework, Stonehouse had closely observed the death of two constituents, and assumed their identities as part of a complex plot to not only commit massive fraud, but to begin a new life abroad with his beautiful Commons secretary, Sheila Buckley. Mrs Stonehouse returned to England, and sued for divorce.

Although he was extradited to Britain, Stonehouse was not expelled by the Labour Party (which at that time had a majority of just three). He continued to hold his seat in the Commons from the confines of a cell in HMP Brixton, and was supported by many MPs, including some Conservatives. However, he was found guilty of fraud in 1976 and sentenced to seven years in prison, finally resigning both his seat and his privy counsellorship. On his release, Stonehouse married Miss Buckley, and turned to writing novels and manufacturing electronic safes.

'Randy old sod'.

The Rt Hon John Prescott

(b.1938) Labour, Hull East 1970–

ABC ⊙⊙

Well, where to begin? Prescott, the Baldrick of New Labour, represents in our view a level of failure rarely surpassed in British politics. The statistics of his spell in government tell their own story: on entering the Cabinet in 1997, he was given a 'super ministry' with a budget of billions of pounds and a staff of several thousand civil servants. But so bad was he at running a department, it seems, that by 2006, he was left with a staff of just eighteen. The news that it once cost £645 to change the sign outside his door from 'Office of the Deputy Prime Minister's suggested to many that Prescott's governmental posts had only ever been created to accommodate his ego.

There was, of course, the trouble with language: 'The government intend to reduce and probably eliminate the homeless by 2008'. He baffled US Vice President Al Gore with his theories on 'the Balklands', and once simply gave up in the middle of a BBC interview, asking if he could start again because he had 'made that crap'. 'We're live, Mr Prescott,' came the response.

It strikes us that Prescott's chief weakness was his enlarged sense of self-importance, and that he never realized the extent to which he was used by New Labour as the fig leaf behind which Tony Blair's Islington trendiness could hide. Such political naivety inevitably damaged his reputation. He was, for example, unaware that using a car to travel just 250 yards from his hotel to give a conference speech on the benefits of public transport might not look good, or that being seen playing croquet on one of the few days Blair dared to leave him in charge of the country might be damaging. And it seems he was prepared to risk everything for an affair with his diary secretary, Tracey Temple, despite the fact that, being a diary secretary, she was recording every detail of the relationship in, yes, her diary. She wrote that he was '…a randy old sod at times coz he wanted sex again…He was so up for it…' He was once 'up for it' after a remembrance service at St Paul's, and Temple, whom he had taken to the service, duly obliged. In fact, she even obliged him in his office, when he was 'going through his ministerial box – maybe things to do with regeneration, or the environment.' He seems to prove the theory that the worst MPs are those who are so blinded by the importance of their position that they become isolated from reality. The deeper mystery with Prescott is how he ever got to that position in the first place. History will look at him, and scratch its head.

Prisoner No. CB9298.

Jonathan Aitken

(b.1942) Conservative, Thanet East 1974–83,
Thanet South 1983–97

Every now and then an MP spectacularly self-destructs in a supernova of shame and disgrace. Britons love this, and never more so than when the hapless victim is a Tory. John Major's government of the 1990s supplied an unusually high number of such figures, and chief among the purveyors of Tory 'sleaze' was Jonathan Aitken.

On 10 April 1995, Aitken stood up in front of a packed press conference and delivered a dramatic statement. In a speech that would have done justice to a Hollywood film, he denounced Granada Television and the *Guardian* newspaper for detailing alleged links with the arms industry and Saudi Arabia, which he angrily denied. 'If it falls to me', he announced, 'to start a fight to cut out the cancer of bent and twisted journalism in our country', then his weapons would be 'the simple sword of truth, and the trusty shield of fair play…I am ready for the fight.' The problem was that his defence also owed as much to fiction as any Hollywood screenplay.

Aitken was then in the Cabinet, but his Commons career had, in fact, started badly. Shortly after his first election in 1974, he made a lifelong enemy of his party leader, Margaret Thatcher, by rather injudiciously dumping her daughter, Carol. He was referred to in the Thatcher household as 'the man who made Carol cry', and left on the backbenches for eighteen years. But to the rescue of his career came an unlikely champion, John Major. In 1992, following the most surprising election victory since Edward Heath's similarly charisma-free triumph, Major rewarded the loyal, well-connected Aitken with the job of Minister for Defence Procurement. In 1994, Aitken joined the Cabinet as Chief Secretary to the Treasury.

However, in October 1994, the *Guardian* newspaper published a number of allegations about Aitken. The newspaper revealed that, in 1993, he had stayed at the Ritz Hotel in Paris, that unhappy nexus of British tragedy, and that it seemed his bill had been paid by Said Ayas, an aide to the Saudi royal family. Given the Saudi involvement in arms contracts, should the then Minister for Defence Procurement have been accepting a gift in this way?

That, Aitken explained, was not a problem, because it had all been a mistake and his wife, Lolicia, had paid back the money. She had travelled to Paris from Switzerland, where his daughter was at school, and then stayed on at the Ritz when he left. Aitken said that a nephew of Ayas had paid their bill in error, and Mrs Aitken's cash had resolved the matter. The Cabinet Secretary investigated and it seemed that Aitken had done nothing wrong. What was more, it emerged that the *Guardian* had used a so-called 'cod' fax, printed on House of Commons paper and purporting to be from Aitken's office, in order to obtain a copy of the hotel bill. Peter Preston, the editor, was dragged before the Commons to be ritually denounced by angry Tory MPs.

Nevertheless, facing more allegations from the *Guardian* and Granada Television, Aitken decided to resign from the Cabinet in July 1995 and to clear his name. He sued both organizations for libel. But in just the second week of the case, his sword of truth began to look a little rusty. It was revealed that, while at the Ritz, and at the time when his wife was supposedly on her way to meet him and pay his bill, Aitken had telephoned the hotel room in Switzerland where she had been staying. Could Mrs Aitken have been in two places at once? Aitken claimed that it was his mother-in-law who had answered the phone. But hadn't the hotel bill from Switzerland shown that his wife had been the only occupant of the room? No matter, said Aitken, for he had corroborating witness statements ready from his unimpeachable daughter, Victoria.

Then, dramatically, new evidence arrived in court. The defendants had discovered car hire details and flight coupons proving that neither Aitken's wife or daughter had been in

France at all. Two days later, the case against the *Guardian* was dropped. 'He lied and lied and lied', read the newspaper's headline the next day. More damning still, he had also asked his daughter and wife to lie in court on his behalf. Aitken became only the third man in the twentieth century to resign his privy counsellorship, following those other brave champions of truth and fair play, John Profumo and John Stonehouse. Aitken was arrested and charged with perjury and perverting the course of justice. His daughter was also arrested, but released without charge. On 8 June 1999, Aitken was convicted on both counts and sentenced to eighteen months in prison.

The most tragic thing about Aitken is that he was pointlessly dishonest. Had he admitted to simply enjoying a free stay at the Ritz, he would have been guilty only of naivety. His case proves the adage that, as President Nixon is reported to have said, 'it's the lie that gets you'. It is a theory Atiken should have been familiar with – he wrote a biography of Nixon in 1993.

'There was no impropriety whatsoever in my acquaintanceship with Miss Keeler'.

John Profumo

(1915–2006) Conservative, Kettering 1940–5, Stratford-on-Avon 1950–63

John Profumo was known as an excellent MP and an admirable Secretary of State for War until 11.00 a.m. on 22 March 1963, when he told the most sensational lie that modern politics had ever heard. In doing so, he unleashed one of the greatest political scandals yet seen in Britain. He was the first to prove that it is not necessarily the crime that gets you – the affair, the fraud, the mistake – but the lie.

Profumo had had a brief affair with Christine Keeler, an escort he had met at Cliveden, country home of the Astors. As was the way in pre-tabloid Britain, Profumo's liaison became known to those 'in-the-know', but little was reported in the mainstream press. At first, Profumo denied having an affair and lied repeatedly to his colleagues, including to the Chief Whip. He probably would have survived, but for the fact that he repeated the lie in the Commons, adding, for good measure: 'I shall not hesitate to issue writs for libel and slander if scandalous allegations are made or repeated outside the House'.

Profumo thus broke the cardinal rule of Parliament – never mislead the House. When the lie was inevitably revealed, Profumo suffered the sort of rapid disgrace which in the past would have seen him end up on Tower Hill: he was forced to surrender his seals of office to the Queen by messenger, rather than in person, as was customary; he was immediately 'resigned' from the Commons, which judged him to have been in contempt; and he surrendered his membership of the Privy Council.

'The Profumo Affair' as it came to be known, was the first great scandal of modern politics, and revolutionized the way in which politicians were viewed by both press and public. Mockery and satire became the order of the day as people wondered what the governing class really got up to. The famous phrase attributed to Macmillan, 'We've never had it so good', was corrupted to 'We've never had it so often'. Parliament suffered a loss of respect that it has never quite regained, and it is for that reason Profumo earns his high ranking here.

3

'Tired and emotional'.

Rt Hon George Brown,
Lord George-Brown

(1914–85) Labour, Belper 1945–70

The post of Deputy Leader of the Labour Party seems to have a strange effect on some of its holders. Perhaps it is the frustration of having such a grand title but no power, or the knowledge that the word 'deputy' is meaningless. For George Brown, who was Deputy Leader for ten years, it was his perpetual failure to gain any real power that led him to despair, drink and self-destruction.

Brown's career in the Commons began well, and in 1960 he succeeded Aneurin Bevan as Deputy Leader. But Brown had an acute weakness for alcohol, and while it aided his ability to make a rousing speech, it impaired his ability to do anything else. 'I have never', wrote Lady Violet Bonham Carter after meeting him, 'met anyone so completely un-house-trained'.

In office Brown was a disaster, habitually drunk from seeking solace in alcohol for the perceived slights and insults of his colleagues. He regularly leaked governmental secrets, bullied his staff, wept in meetings and once publicly resigned and unresigned himself from the Cabinet in the space of twenty-four hours, to the astonishment of the then Prime Minister, Harold Wilson.

Brown's staff, who coined the famous phrase 'tired and emotional' as a euphemism for his intoxication, used to make pretend 'drinks' for whomever joined him for meetings so that he didn't feel out of place with his own large whiskies, particularly before lunch.

Brown held two Cabinet posts, at the Department for Economic Affairs from 1964–6 and at the Foreign Office from 1966–8. His Foreign Secretary credentials were already poor, for he was well known for his drunken appearance on national television following the assassination of President Kennedy in 1963, flamboyantly mourning the loss of someone he claimed was among his best friends, despite having only met him three times. He was particularly disliked by Britain's ambassadors, for if he thought their wives were too old or too ugly he would say so, believing they gave a bad impression of Britain. The story of him mistaking the Cardinal Archbishop of Montevideo for a woman and asking him to dance during the Peruvian national anthem is apocryphal, but that of him leaving a top secret document in the back of a car he had drunkenly hitchhiked in at 3.00 a.m. is true. The document was 'The National Plan', the big idea of Brown's Cabinet career which, according to one of Brown's colleagues, 'sank without trace within minutes of its being completed'. By an odd coincidence, Brown's namesake, Gordon, launched his own 'National Plan' in the summer of 2009. Will it share the same fate?

Rant.

Sir Oswald Mosley

(1896–1980) Harrow 1918–24,
Birmingham Smethwick 1926–31

The handsome scion of an old Staffordshire family, in another age Sir Oswald Mosley might have been a typical Conservative squire. And, at the outset of his political career in 1918, that was precisely what he was. He was wooed by society and by the glamorous women he met at its gatherings, many of whom he bedded. He had a solid war record and was elected at the youthful age of twenty-two as Unionist MP for Harrow. However, Mosley was perpetually impatient, ambitious and unfaithful, craving attention and power. His first wife, Lady Cynthia Mosley, got a taste of his infidelity in their brief, uncomfortable marriage, before she died in 1933.

It was his political infidelity, however, that increasingly brought him into the national spotlight. Having fallen out with the Conservative Party, he declared himself an Independent in 1920, and in 1924, he joined the Labour Party. Winning a by-election in 1926, he became a prominent Labour MP, and then a minister in Ramsay MacDonald's Labour government of 1929. But he was frustrated at only being given the junior job of Chancellor of the Duchy of Lancaster. In 1930, he resigned in protest at the government's failure to listen to his ideas for dealing with the economic crisis. He decided to form a new party, which he named – with great originality – the New Party. It was astonishingly unsuccessful.

The New Party failed to win any seats at the only election it fought, so Mosley came up with another plan to promote his restless ego: the British Union of Fascists. Given Mussolini's success in Italy, fascism seemed to Mosley the obvious next choice. When he married one of the Mitford sisters, Diana, their wedding guests included Adolf Hitler. The BUF adopted black-shirt uniforms and marched against communism. But there were significant problems with Mosley's plan: Britain was not Germany, Mosley was not Hitler and the National Government was not the failed government of Weimar Germany. 'Hail Mosley' was probably the least successful political slogan in history.

The BUF became increasingly anti-Semitic, lost the backing of its powerful supporters and even embroiled itself in street battles. Mosley was increasingly irrelevant in British politics. When war came, he was interned. After the war, his anti-immigration campaigns were as ill-judged as his pre-war ones. Mosley was not very interested in Parliament, his constituents or, perhaps, even in politics. Mosley was interested in himself.

Sir Edward Grey,
Viscount Grey of Fallodon

(1862–1933) Liberal, Berwick-upon-Tweed 1885–1916

On 3 August 1914, Foreign Secretary Sir Edward Grey stood up in the House of Commons and delivered the best speech of his career: he announced that Britain would enter the First World War. It was probably the worst decision in modern British history.

Grey had been Foreign Secretary since 1905 and his appointment had been something of a surprise. He never really liked being an MP (instead preferring fishing), and his only previous government post was the minor job of Under Secretary for Foreign Affairs. But despite a reputation for idleness and indolence (for which he had been sent down from Oxford), he stayed at the Foreign Office until 1916.

The crucial mistakes of Grey's spell as Foreign Secretary were made early on. First, he allowed the relatively innocuous Anglo–French entente of 1904 to develop into a quasi-military alliance with the French. He and the Prime Minister, Herbert Asquith, decided not to trouble the rest of the Cabinet about Britain's secret military talks. Second, Grey agreed to the 1907 Anglo–Russian entente, partly because he feared (incorrectly, since Russia had just been soundly beaten by the Japanese) that Russia was strong enough to threaten Britain's interests in India and the Middle East. As a result, the impression was gradually given to France and Russia that Britain was an ally and could be relied upon in the event of war. Under Grey, Britain effectively joined the system of modern European military alliances for the first time.

Previously, Britain had always tried to remain aloof. We intervened occasionally, and only then very reluctantly, only if

83

Continued

the 'Balance of Power' seemed tilted too far in favour of any single Power. But in general, Britain looked disdainfully across the Channel and tried to ignore our squabbling European relations. We had done so since Henry VIII first broke free from Rome, and we continue to do so today by remaining outside the Euro. Such a policy is caricatured as one of 'isolation', but in Grey's time it was probably better described as non-intervention. As one of Grey's predecessors as Foreign Secretary, the 15th Earl Derby, pointed out in 1877, 'as long as our own interests are not touched, why should not foreigners settle their own affairs in their own way?'

Grey's decision, therefore, marked a watershed in British foreign policy. Not since the days of Waterloo almost a century earlier had Britain intervened militarily in Europe on such a major scale. Then, Napoleon had threatened to rampage across the continent, and had proved the nature of his threat to this country by amassing a large invasion fleet in the Channel. But in 1914, the threat to Britain was not immediately obvious. Europe was on the brink of war for the most trivial reason: just weeks earlier, the nephew of the Austrian emperor was assassinated in Sarajevo by disgruntled Serbs. The Austrians immediately threatened to retaliate against Serbia, but — and this is where matters became complicated — Serbia enjoyed the protection of Russia, and Russia threatened to invade Austria if Serbia was attacked. Austria, however, had the protection of Germany, and Germany threatened to attack Russia if Austria was invaded. Finally, Russia had the support of France, and France threatened to invade Germany if Russia was attacked. In quick succession Austria, Russia, Germany and France mobilized their armies and invoked the treaties and secret alliances which, ostensibly, were meant to act as a brake against war.

But while each individual step was itself defensive, together they appeared to nervous politicians and generals to be offensive, and so, by a process of ineptitude and miscommunication, Europe rolled helplessly towards collision.

But there was still little indication that any of this drama involved Britain. Germany had never been our enemy. There is no evidence that in 1914 Germany wished to fight a war of occupation in Europe, or intended to invade Britain. Our historical ties to Germany (not least through our monarchy) were stronger than our ties to France, against whom we had fought countless wars. And when France and Germany had last gone to war, in 1870, the French had been comprehensively beaten, and nobody in Britain was the least bothered. If anyone was our 'enemy' it was Russia, whom we had fought during the Crimean War of 1854–6, and very nearly again in 1878.

Grey, who had never liked the Germans and disliked the notion of Britain being left 'isolated', nonetheless presented his colleagues with a compelling reason for Britain to join the fray. And what was this vital interest so close to the hearts of everyone in Britain? It was, of course, Belgium. In 1839, Britain, along with the rest of Europe, had signed a treaty guaranteeing to protect Belgium's integrity. In August 1914, long after the treaty had ceased to be a central foundation of European geopolitics, Germany refused to guarantee Belgium's independence, because under their military plans part of the German army would cross Belgian territory on its way into France. Many of Grey's Liberal colleagues were against intervening on Belgium's behalf, such as Lloyd George, the then Chancellor, who pointed out that Germany would merely march through the southernmost point of Belgium. 'You see', he said, pointing at a map, 'it is only a little bit, and the Germans will pay for any damage they do.' But for Grey and Asquith, Belgium was the excuse needed to mobilize the largely anti-war Liberal Party behind the decision to go to war, and so maintain the Liberal government. At Grey's behest, the Cabinet reluctantly agreed that its obligations under the 1839 treaty compelled Britain to fight.

In his famous speech in the Commons Grey justified his decision thus: 'If, in a crisis like this, we run away from those obligations of honour and interest as regards the Belgian Treaty, I doubt whether, whatever material force we might have at the end, it would be of very much value in face of the respect that we should have lost.' Did Britain really have to suffer 2.3 million

Continued

casualties, bankrupt herself and hasten the loss of her empire, simply to preserve respect and honour?

Grey was a tragic figure. He later went blind, and after his retirement, lived a sad life wondering if the events of 1914 might have been handled differently. It is hard not to feel sorry for him. He was in the wrong place at the wrong time, and it is, of course, wrong to accuse him of causing all the death and horror of the First World War – that honour belongs chiefly to the generals, the 'donkeys', on both sides. Others, too, not least Asquith, deserve equal censure for Britain's decision to declare war. But in August 1914, Britain needed decisive leadership in its foreign policy if it was to secure peace, and instead she drifted into war. Some may wonder why Grey is included in this list for his part in the origins of the First World War, and not Neville Chamberlain for his part in the origins of the Second World War. The answer is simple: Chamberlain tried to keep Britain out of war, but failed. Grey tried to take Britain into war, and succeeded. For that reason, he deserves his special place here. He is proof that, although we can laugh at crap MPs, sometimes they rise to the top and make mistakes that affect us all.

Picture Credits

4. PA Wire/Press Association Images; 5. Guildhall Library, City of London/ The Bridgeman Art Library; 6. Getty Images; 7. Time & Life Pictures/Getty Images; 8. Rex Features; 9. © 2005 Charles Walker / TopFoto; 10. Bibliotheque Nationale, Paris, France/ The Bridgeman Art Library; 11. Daily Mail / Rex Features; 12. S&G Barratts/Press Association Images; 13. The Granger Collection, New York; 14. © Nicholas Garland, The New Spectator, 14th July 1990, British Cartoon Archive, University of Kent, www. cartoons.ac.uk; 15. PA Wire/Press Association Images; 16. © UPPA/Photoshot; 17. Getty Images; 18. World History Archive / Alamy; 19. © National Portrait Gallery, London; 20. © National Portrait Gallery, London; 21. © National Portrait Gallery, London; 22. DPA/Press Association Images; 24. TopFoto/UPP; 25. Rex Features; 26. Corporation of London/HIP/Topfoto; 27. © National Portrait Gallery, London; 28. © National Portrait Gallery, London; 29. TopFoto/UPP; 30. © National Portrait Gallery, London; 32. Mary Evans Picture Library; 33. © National Portrait Gallery, London; 34. Ian Miles–Flashpoint Pictures/ Alamy; 36. The Parliamentary Archives; 37. Doug Mackenzie / Evening Standard / Rex Features; 39. Getty Images; 40. Getty Images; 42. PA Archive/Press Association Images; 44. Getty Images; 45. Solo ; 47. Getty Images; 48. Print Collector / HIP / TopFoto.